40 Days of Rest

A Lifestyle Soaked in the Peace of God

Seth Jeffery

O&U
Onwards & Upwards

Onwards and Upwards Publishers

4 The Old Smithy, London Road, Rockbeare,
EX5 2EA, United Kingdom.
www.onwardsandupwards.org

Copyright © Seth Jeffery 2021

The moral right of Seth Jeffery to be identified as the author of this work has been asserted by the author in accordance with the Copyright, Designs and Patents Act 1988.

All rights reserved.

No part of this publication may be reproduced or transmitted in any form or by any means, electronic or mechanical, including photocopy, recording or any information storage and retrieval system, without permission in writing from the author or publisher.

First edition, published in the United Kingdom by Onwards and Upwards Publishers (2020).

ISBN:	978-1-78815-511-3
Typeface:	Sabon LT
Graphic design:	LM Graphic Design

The views and opinions expressed in this book are the author's own, and do not necessarily represent the views and opinions of Onwards and Upwards Publishers or its staff.

Scripture quotations marked (AMP) are taken from the Amplified® Bible, Copyright © 2015 by The Lockman Foundation. Used by permission. www.Lockman.org

Scripture quotations marked (ESV) are from the ESV® Bible (The Holy Bible, English Standard Version®), copyright © 2001 by Crossway, a publishing ministry of Good News Publishers. Used by permission. All rights reserved.

Scripture quotations marked (NASB) are taken from the New American Standard Bible® (NASB), Copyright © 1960, 1962, 1963, 1968, 1971, 1972, 1973, 1975, 1977, 1995 by The Lockman Foundation. Used by permission. www.Lockman.org

Scripture quotations marked (NIV) are taken from THE HOLY BIBLE, NEW INTERNATIONAL VERSION®, NIV® Copyright © 1973, 1978, 1984, 2011 by Biblica, Inc.™ Used by permission. All rights reserved worldwide.

Scripture quotations marked (NKJV) are taken from the New King James Version®. Copyright © 1982 by Thomas Nelson. Used by permission. All rights reserved.

Scripture quotations marked (NLT) are taken from the Holy Bible, New Living Translation, copyright © 1996, 2004, 2007, 2013 by Tyndale House Foundation. Used by permission of Tyndale House Publishers, Inc., Carol Stream, Illinois 60188. All rights reserved.

About the Author

Seth is a worship leader and missionary to Europe, currently living in France. He and his wife Ana are passionate about worship, often teaching about maintaining a lifestyle soaked in the presence of God and contending in prayer.

To contact the author, please write to:

Seth Jeffery
c/o Onwards and Upwards Publishers Ltd.
4 The Old Smithy
London Road
Rockbeare
EX5 2EA

Contents

Foreword by Father Antoine Coelho 7
1. Start by Stopping 9
2. Sleep Through the Storm 11
3. Speak to the Rock 13
4. You Have God's Attention 15
5. The First Year of Marriage 17
6. Night to Day 19
7. Contagious Peace 21
8. The Never-Ending Sabbath 23
9. Patience is a Virtue 25
10. Easy Like Sunday Morning 27
11. Be Still and Know You're Not God 29
12. Rest's Greatest Enemy 31
13. Action and Reaction 33
14. Soaking 35
15. Coping Perfectly 37
16. Vengeance is Not Yours 39
17. Own the Day, Relinquish the Night 41
18. Anti-Aging Secrets 43
19. Morning Joy 45
20. Knowing Your Place 47

21. Smart Economics 49
22. No Compromise 51
23. Let It Go! 53
24. Refreshing Repentance 55
25. Faith Like Flowers 57
26. God is There in Your Darkest Place 59
27. The Best-Laid Plans 61
28. Friendships, Not Followers 63
29. Let the Anointing Flow 65
30. Watch and Learn 67
31. Eat, Drink, Be Merry 69
32. The Karma of Queuing 71
33. Living for Today 73
34. Pay Off Your Procrastination 75
35. Your Angelic Entourage 77
36. Refresh Your Memory 79
37. A Table Awaits 81
38. Climate Change 83
39. Creation's Testimony 85
40. Silence! 87

Foreword

I thank the Lord for having inspired Seth to write this little book on the Christian concept of rest. I have to say, I find it often difficult to rest, being so involved in the ministry and knowing how important it is to help people get saved and give their lives to the Lord.

More and more the Lord has been speaking to me about the power of rest, peace and trust. Lately it has become a major topic in my preaching. That's why I find it so providential to have this booklet in my hands. It's a fact that God fights our battles but it's also very clear that He's most of the time invisible and fights them in ways we don't expect and according to a calendar we don't control.

So instead of letting God do it with our cooperation, we tend very easily to take His place and try ourselves to do it with His cooperation. This can work for a time, but not for your whole life. Sooner or later deep tiredness and frustration will come, and perhaps even desperation.

The fact is that we have been taught to work, to work for the Lord or to work for money, but we haven't been always taught to rest, and perhaps even less to rest in the Lord. I see Seth's book as a most valuable contribution to this important cause, offering you a forty-day journey through the biblical and Christian concept of rest. I strongly advise you not to rush through these pages, but to read them and to pray them – why not – in forty days! Big lessons need some time to be assimilated.

Father Antoine Coelho
Holy Spirit House

1

Start by Stopping

By the seventh day God had finished the work he had been doing; so on the seventh day he rested from all his work.

Genesis 2:2 (NIV)

Whether you believe in a literal seven-day creation or not, what's important here is what Genesis teaches us about God's nature and His relationship with His creation.

We know that the LORD rested on the seventh day and from there gave us the demonstration of the Sabbath rest – the word 'Sabbath' deriving from the Hebrew word *sabat* meaning 'to stop or cease'. We also know that before the seventh day, mankind was the last thing that He created.

So, consider for a moment that God did not create man first and ask him to then help with the rest of the work. By the time man was formed, all the work of creation was complete, and the only day left was the day of rest. The LORD's seventh day is our first day. Therefore, do not see rest as a far-off destination to recover at, but the place you start from, filling your tank up before setting out. Rest and relationship are not the end but the beginning, for God has already prepared them for you.

Pray today...

Father God, I'm taking this moment now to stop, and acknowledge that, as with Adam and Eve, You prepared everything before I even took my first breath. I'm choosing to work from a place of rest and relationship, and to always give from a filled cup. Let your Sabbath be the place I start from, and may I also provide a place of rest for others to start from.

2

Sleep Through the Storm

Jesus was in the stern, sleeping on a cushion. The disciples woke him and said to him, "Teacher, don't you care if we drown?" He got up, rebuked the wind and said to the waves, "Quiet! Be still!" Then the wind died down and it was completely calm.

Mark 4:38-39 (NIV)

The peace of God surpasses understanding – that is, it simply doesn't make sense to those around. Jesus exemplified peace, because he was completely unmoved by storms in a way that shocked His disciples.

Jesus could have kept sleeping if He wanted to. His perfect peace was not to prevent storms from happening, but to be undisturbed by them. This is the peace that the Holy Spirit produces in you. Had the disciples not been there to awaken Him, it seems unlikely that Jesus would even have felt a need to change the atmosphere.

However, the fact that He did calm the storm shows a beautiful depth of the peace of God: that it can break in from the spiritual into the physical in order to bring peaceful atmospheres for others who need help. That might be through a command like Jesus before his disciples, or it could even be through a musical instrument like David before King Saul. So even if a thousand may fall at your side, if you seek the peace of God embodied in Christ Jesus, you will not be moved, but will be the movement.

Pray today...

Holy Spirit, I want You to grow more peace in my life. Teach me how to sleep peacefully through the storms in my own life and to bring perfect peace into the lives of those around me.

3

Speak to the Rock

"Take the staff, and you and your brother Aaron gather the assembly together. Speak to that rock before their eyes and it will pour out its water. You will bring water out of the rock for the community so that they and their livestock can drink."

Numbers 20:8 (NIV)

The first time that Moses brought water from the rock, he was commanded to strike it. The second time, the LORD was bringing him to a higher level of trust, so He commanded him to merely speak to the rock.

God is always calling His people to higher levels of faith and rest, where we are commanding His blessing instead of striving or striking for it. In fact, the greatest faith Jesus said He had ever seen was a Roman centurion who believed that a single word of authority was enough for healing power to be released.

In Numbers 20 we see the LORD's reaction to Moses' preference to keep striking instead of speaking. Moses had chosen not to step up into a place of rest, and as a result he could not enter the promised land, a symbol of rest. Do not be tempted to believe your miracle must always come from striking, for the LORD's destiny for you is to step up into restful authority.

Pray today...

Heavenly Father, please give me the faith and trust to step up into the realm of restful authority You have for me. Show me areas of my life where I've hung on to human effort and formulae. I have nothing to prove to anyone, I just want to enter into your rest and your will.

4

You Have God's Attention

Because He has inclined His ear to me,
Therefore I shall call upon Him as long as I live.
                                              Psalm 116:2 (NASB)

It is not certain which occasion caused David to pen Psalm 116, or whether it was simply a reaction to a life of seeing the LORD's faithfulness and forgiveness. Either way, he shares an encouraging and exciting revelation to all believers: you always have God's attention.

The conclusion that David comes to is not to try calling upon the LORD from time to time to test if He might decide to listen again. Rather, his resolve is to call upon the LORD as long as he lives, safe in the knowledge that He is unchanging, and therefore always listening.

While there is a time for warfare and intercession, we should not expect to constantly pound our fists on the floor and wail ourselves to exhaustion in order to reach a faraway god. You can rest in the knowledge that the LORD is close and always listening. Remember: if He spoke to Elijah with a still, small voice, He is just as ready to hear your own still, small voice.

Pray today...

LORD God, I'm fully aware of You, and I know that You are also fully aware of me. I want to engage in conversation even more sincerely and regularly to You, knowing that You are always listening intently and are ready to guide me through every circumstance.

5

The First Year of Marriage

> *When a man has taken a new wife, he shall not go out to war or be charged with any business; he shall be free at home one year, and bring happiness to his wife whom he has taken.*
>
> Deuteronomy 24:5 (NKJV)

When people read this passage, there are reactions from "Wow!" to "No way is that doable!" But it's true, the Mosaic law stipulates that the first task for a newly married couple is to stay at home, rest and enjoy each other for a year. The LORD knows that the best way to build strong, long-lasting relationships is through setting aside intentional quality time together before having to respond to a call of duty.

This may all seem like an unrealistic scenario given today's financial pressures, and indeed it may be hard if not impossible for many young couples to simply stop working. However, there is a deeper lesson here.

Whenever we establish new friendships, connections, or join a new congregation, there can be pressure to get to work quickly. In fact, the church's culture may even promote it, especially if one's gifts are evident. But God teaches us to value friendship before function. So, before you go out to fight battles and build kingdoms, make sure you set aside an intentional season to build deep, long-lasting connections.

Pray today...

Dear Jesus, help me with my priorities. Show me if I have neglected relationships by jumping to work too quickly. Today, I choose to first enjoy and build strong relationships, before building strong kingdoms.

6

Night to Day

The way of the righteous is like the first gleam of dawn, which shines ever brighter until the full light of day.

Proverbs 4:18 (NLT)

In the calendar which we typically use, a day lasts from midnight to midnight. But the Bible teaches us different timekeeping: a day lasts from sundown to sundown.

This is an object lesson about the nature of progression. Your destiny in Christ is not to end each season of life at midnight, in dark and sorrowful circumstances; it is to seek His righteousness and to be transformed into His likeness with ever-increasing glory.

Just as the Biblical day starts in the evening and is destined to see the sunrise, so you can trust that God's plan for your life is always to bring things out of darkness and into light. Sorrow may last for the night, but as a child of the day (see 1 Thessalonians 5:5) your destiny is not to stay there, but to follow the first gleam of dawn, shining brighter until the full light of day.

Pray today...

LORD, You are my light and my salvation. Increase my faith to live as a child of the day. Even when I feel that I am in a night season, I know that the story will not end there, for You will lead me to awaken the dawn and to see Your glory.

7

Contagious Peace

"I am leaving you with a gift—peace of mind and heart. And the peace I give is a gift the world cannot give. So don't be troubled or afraid."

John 14:27 (NLT)

Several years ago, a friend of mine told me that he had once received a blessing of peace from a mentor, which had never left him. He then proceeded to lay hands on me and impart that same peace.

Have you noticed that the peace of God is very transferrable? Certainly, people who live with stress seem to pass it around wherever they go! The Hebrews understood this power, greeting everyone with *shalom*. Peace was one of the few things, apart from the Holy Spirit, that Jesus explicitly imparted to His disciples.

Atmospheres of peace and stress are clearly contagious, as we have all seen. They spread their calm or panic for a moment before then lifting. But here is the beauty of the peace that Jesus gives: it is of His own nature, which means that it cannot leave you, nor forsake you. The more you turn your awareness to Jesus, the more you will see His peace grow in your life as it becomes a part of you, a peace you can transfer to others.

Pray today...

Jesus, You are the Prince of Peace. I receive Your peace forever, and I'm reminded that it will never leave me. Teach me how to walk in it every day, and how to transfer it to others, for Your glory.

8

The Never-Ending Sabbath

Then God blessed the seventh day and sanctified it, because in it He rested from all His work which God had created and made.

Genesis 2:3 (NASB)

Every day of creation ends with the same statement, that there was evening, and there was morning, and that was the nth day. Only one day doesn't end this way: the day of rest. In fact, it doesn't have an explicit ending at all.

The verse says that God blessed the day. Think about this for a moment: the creator of the universe laying hands on and blessing time itself. This Sabbath day is blessed to be a blessing to all who receive it, and because the day is given no end, that blessing is always available.

We may live in seven-day cycles of weekdays and weekends, but whether you are able or not to mark a dedicated day where you can switch off from work, the blessing of the Sabbath is not confined to a single weekday. Sabbath-rest is never-ending, it is available every time you step into a place of choosing relationship with God. That time you put aside for Him has been blessed since creation, and its nature is to bless you too.

Pray today...

Thank You, Father, for blessing this time and setting it for eternity. Being with You right now is Sabbath rest. No matter how busy life gets, I choose to always make today the day of relationship with You.

9

Patience is a Virtue

> *My brethren, count it all joy when you fall into various trials, knowing that the testing of your faith produces patience. But let patience have its perfect work, that you may be perfect and complete, lacking nothing.*
>
> James 1:2-4 (NKJV)

I once heard a preacher jokingly say, "Don't ask the LORD for patience because you'll regret what He will put you through to produce it." I must assume he was joking because this can never be our disposition! Patience is one of the great fruits the Holy Spirit will produce in you, and God's desire is for it to bring blessing and fullness, not pain or suffering.

Patience does, of course, come through enduring challenges, as James writes, and while this may seem a strange thing to encourage in a devotional of rest and peace, growing the fruit of patience now will allow you to persevere and find rest in the midst of any future trial.

Note that patience does not come to us by looking for trouble, but when trouble does come, by looking ahead towards perseverance. So earnestly desire patience, because the Word promises it will make you "perfect and complete, lacking nothing" – what an invaluable gift that is!

Pray today...

Holy Spirit, I invite You to grow patience in my life. Whenever challenges come, I choose to be grateful of the opportunity to persevere, yet please help me in those occasions to always keep my eyes looking ahead.

10

Easy Like Sunday Morning

*"Just say a simple, 'Yes, I will,' or 'No, I won't.'
Anything beyond this is from the evil one."*

Matthew 5:37 (NLT)

Do you know someone who frustrates you when they speak because you can never be sure what they mean by what they say? Perhaps they are hard to count on, or they are the kind of person that you always have to read between the lines to decipher their true intent.

One of the simplest, most practical strategies for having an easier and more peaceful life, is to be as uncomplicated as possible. If you want to pay for someone's meal, go for it! If they want to pay for yours, let them! This was one of the best personal decisions I remember making, as life instantly became smoother not just for me but for my friends too!

It's so easy to adopt a false humility that is really pride. Instead, let your words be straightforward, and your motives pure, then just trust the Holy Spirit to help put it together. Suddenly, what were once complicated social interactions and hidden intentions are now gracious opportunities for love and blessing to flow!

Pray today...

LORD, I don't want to complicate things. I would rather do everything with pure motives, so that my lips are clean, and so that Your peace and blessings can flow. I commit to being trustworthy, someone that others can count on to speak the truth with no reservation or hidden agenda.

11

Be Still and Know You're Not God

Be still, and know that I am God;
I will be exalted among the nations,
I will be exalted in the earth!

Psalm 46:10 (NKJV)

The Bible commands us to be completely still. Here's the thing about being completely still: you cannot do anything! You are unable to get involved and take control of the situation.

When we desire to control things, it is a form of godship. God is sovereign, which means He is fully in control. If I want to be the one in control over something, then I am taking the place of God.

Is there something weighing on your mind? Are there activities you feel the need to have a say on or control over? Be still, because by doing so you are acknowledging that you are not sovereign. This will not only allow God to display His sovereignty instead, but it will also give you access to His peace.

Is this lazy? No, the difference between being still and being lazy is simply one of motive. Being lazy is desiring not to work; being still is desiring to let God work.

Pray today...

LORD, You are God and I am not. I give control and management of every situation and task over to You right now. I will quiet my soul and find rest in Your sovereignty. I will be still and know that You are God.

12

Rest's Greatest Enemy

For whoever has entered God's rest has also rested from his works as God did from his. Let us therefore strive to enter that rest, so that no one may fall by the same sort of disobedience.

Hebrews 4:10-11 (ESV)

As much as we must rest from striving, we must also strive at resting! This passage in Hebrews delivers an urgency for us to enter God's rest, and also presents its greatest Enemy. This "same sort of disobedience", which we must make every effort not to fall into, was the grumbling of the Israelites. Almost an entire generation traded away their ticket into the Promised Land because of a culture of complaining and devaluing.

Here is a crucial lesson about resting: the Promised Land is a symbol of God's rest, and due to a prevalent culture of ingratitude and indifference, an entire generation failed to inherit it, save for two men. Joshua and Caleb stood out from the entire nation as the only two who saw its value, who strived for it, and who then received it.

If you devalue resting in God, you will forfeit resting in life. But if you esteem it enough to strive for it – if you understand the value of a life of godly rest – you will inherit it, even as all those around you may give up.

Pray today...

Holy Spirit, remind me of the worth of resting in God. Show me how to revere and treasure the times of refreshing, so that I can enjoy more and more the hours spent in the Father's presence. Please give me an accurate understanding of the true value of rest.

13

Action and Reaction

Don't worry about anything; instead, pray about everything. Tell God what you need, and thank him for all he has done.

Philippians 4:6 (NLT)

Isaac Newton's Third Law of Motion is summarized in a well-known and simple principle: that for every action there is an equal and opposite reaction. It means that if I push a large object in one direction, that object is also pushing back at me in the opposite direction and with the same force, and my hand feels the force.

Unlike Newton, God did not discover the laws of motion, He created them! And like so many natural laws that God created, they are lessons to teach us about both natural and spiritual phenomena; as God-ordained laws they teach us how to live well and righteously.

So if circumstances rise up to tempt you into worry and anxiety, your equal-and-opposing force is prayer. If needs rise up and you don't know how you are going to pay the bills, your equal-and-opposing force is thanksgiving. For as much as you feel pressure from any undesirable force, your role is to cancel out that pressure, not with stress or redirection like the world often acts, but with prayer and thanksgiving.

Pray today...

LORD God, whatever worries or needs come my way, I choose to meet them with simple prayer and thanksgiving. I resolve to always let You know what is going on, and I thank You for your unfailing goodness which I can hold on to and declare in the face of any pressure.

14

Soaking

"Now bring me someone who can play the harp."
While the harp was being played, the power of the
*L*ORD *came upon Elisha.*

2 Kings 3:15 (NLT)

The idea of playing 'soaking music' in order to draw closer to God may seem like a modern trend, but it has been practised since ancient times; only the style and instrumentation have changed to reflect musical trends. Whether it is a psalmist quietening his soul, a young boy David playing to relax the king's tormented mind, or a nameless harpist serving under a prophet, music has often been employed to bring a powerful atmosphere and help us to focus on the voice of the LORD.

When my wife and I used to serve in a healing ministry, the entire team would all sit in silence, eyes closed, with worship music playing for two hours. At first, we were not used to this format – wondering if some even used it as an excuse to get a little sleep – but the results spoke for themselves as accurate prophetic words and pictures were shared immediately after the soaking time, leading to many healings.

If you are not used to soaking, or only have seen it employed in a church service context, make it a lifestyle choice from today. Set a regular time to eliminate distractions and let the Father's love wash over you.

Pray today...

Father God, I receive Your love and I want to hear Your voice clearly. Help me to lay aside distractions and set apart a time just to listen to You.

15

Coping Perfectly

Then Jesus said, "Come to me, all of you who are weary and carry heavy burdens, and I will give you rest. Take my yoke upon you. Let me teach you, because I am humble and gentle at heart, and you will find rest for your souls."

Matthew 11:28-29 (NLT)

Life has its fair share of burdens; fractured relationships, guilt, anger, painful processes, to name a few. We soon discover coping mechanisms that allow us to soften the pain of hardships or to ignore them altogether.

Some people turn to alcohol in order to forget pain, for others it can be pornography. Video games and films also have the ability to distract us from weariness and can become subtly addictive. And there are those who turn to people, texting or calling a best friend for long hours in order to offload all their problems on to them.

All these coping mechanisms have something in common: they help us to temporarily forget our pain, but without confronting or healing it.

Jesus presents the real solution: bring your heavy burdens to Him. He does not promise to remove them or to make you forget them, but instead promises to teach you gently, so you can find the peace, strength and direction to address any and all burdens, and bring them to rest.

Pray today...

Jesus, I am sorry for the coping mechanisms I've turned to. Instead, I am going to come directly to You with life's hardships and pain. I accept Your direction, Your teaching, and I receive Your easy yoke.

16

Vengeance is Not Yours

Do not take revenge, my dear friends, but leave room for God's wrath, for it is written: "It is mine to avenge; I will repay," says the LORD.
Romans 12:19 (NIV)

In most stories, we expect an ending where the hero wins, and the villain receives their appropriate punishment. It fits with our innate sense of justice. But sadly, real life doesn't always turn out this way. So what is your reaction when someone wrongs you but goes unpunished?

It might be as simple as someone cutting in line, driving irresponsibly; or it might be as painful as theft, assault, or death. Whatever wrong you might receive, scripture exhorts us to let God be the one to dispense justice. By stepping back, you give God permission to step in, and it proves that you do trust Him. He will give you peace, as well as full repayment on top.

This doesn't mean that Christians shouldn't bring evil into the light or stand up for the weak, nor does it mean to be a pushover. Rather, it is about knowing who you are and who your Father is. He is fully able and willing to do all that is necessary to avenge and to repay what is stolen from His children, so let's let Him be the one to do it.

Pray today...

LORD, You are my judge and my deliverer. I trust You to do everything necessary to bring justice and revenge when I am wronged. Even if it's different to what I would do, I still trust You, because I know that You are the perfect Judge and God, full of justice and mercy.

17

Own the Day, Relinquish the Night

You are all children of the light and children of the day. We do not belong to the night or to the darkness.

                                    1 Thessalonians 5:5 (NIV)

On the first day, God separated light from darkness, calling the light "Day" and the darkness "Night". This is more than just an explanation of how God created the physical world; it also describes how He created the spiritual world, and its nature.

As children of the light, we have an affinity to the day. We belong to it, and it to us. Just as the Sabbath was made for man, to be a blessing, so daytime was also created as the ideal home for children of the light.

When we make things practical – like water baptism, raising our hands, bowing down – we receive them by faith with all their blessings. So consider what practical steps you might take to own the day instead of the world's tendency to embrace the night. It may be changing sleep patterns in order to wake up early and get more physical rest at night, or it may mean altering your routine to make the most of the daylight.

If owning the day seems impossible because of night shifts, or if you have always seen yourself as a 'night owl' who performs best after sundown, receive the word and pray to the God of the impossible, that He will supply your every need for you to live in the blessing of the day.

Pray today...

God, You created the light to be my home. Show me now the steps I can take today to own my identity as a child of the day.

18

Anti-Aging Secrets

Even youths grow tired and weary, and young men stumble and fall; but those who hope in the LORD will renew their strength. They will soar on wings like eagles; they will run and not grow weary, they will walk and not be faint.

Isaiah 40:30-31 (NIV)

I knew a man of God who amazed us when one day he admitted his age. He had such a youthful vigour and joyful smile that we had always imagined him as someone twenty years younger. More than physical appearances and genes though, I believe it was his bubbling hope in the LORD that made such a difference and came out naturally.

The word that is translated here as "hope" does not mean 'to wish', but rather it means 'to wait, to look upon, or to expect'. The word originally derives from the meaning 'to bind together', as with the waters being gathered together during creation in Genesis 1:9.

Hope in God is not wishful thinking, nor does it mean to wait with uncertainty of the outcome. It is being able to wait with delightful expectation, knowing that your destiny is bound together with God. As you wait upon God with this hopeful certainty, the outcome in your life will be a joy that cannot help but strengthen your bones and radiate from your face.

Pray today...

LORD, my future is bound together with You, as are all my days. Grow in me the deep, joyful assurance of knowing that You have my life, and that You are always working everything for Your glory and my good.

19

Morning Joy

For His anger is but for a moment, his favour is for a lifetime. Weeping may endure for a night, but a shout of joy comes in the morning.

Psalm 30:5 (AMP)

One recent Friday, one of my colleagues at work asked the rest of the team to all send GIFs describing their week and how they were feeling. The group was soon flooded with videos of babies passing out, animals sleeping, people being slapped by fish, and so on. It was all for fun, of course, but the reality of how the world feels about Fridays was clear.

Yet the Bible makes something else clear: your destiny is not to live a life of sorrow and tiredness week after week, interspersed with a few moments of relief. This is the mindset of the world, not the Kingdom. For God's children, weeping is confined to the night – the time that God brings you to rest, not to dwell. Your destiny is therefore to awake with shouts of joy.

You may find in the culture that renewing your mind and declaring God's joy makes you look like a killjoy to those who have not received it. But Jesus insists we "let the dead bury their own dead". There is a shout of joy for you, and a lifetime of favour; may you receive it in Jesus' name!

Pray today...

LORD God, I am ready to go out with a shout of joy today, because I know that You are always good. You take my mourning and turn it into dancing. I declare that You are clothing me with joy and gladness every day.

20

Knowing Your Place

If they had longed for the country they came from, they could have gone back. But they were looking for a better place, a heavenly homeland. That is why God is not ashamed to be called their God, for he has prepared a city for them.

Hebrews 11:15-16 (NLT)

C.S. Lewis wrote in *Mere Christianity*, "If I find in myself a desire which no experience in this world can satisfy, the most probable explanation is that I was made for another world."

The writer of Hebrews, when writing about the heroes of faith, indicates that God prepared a heavenly place for them. As we read the stories of Abraham, Noah, Moses and others, we often see them heading toward a promised land, and while it seemed to be a land here (such as Canaan), God still commended this movement as showing their true heart.

There is great peace and contentment that will fill your heart as you understand that this world and its offerings are not your inheritance, that they cannot ultimately satisfy, and the writing on your passport is more of a visa than a nationality. You are not a 'citizen of the world' but an ambassador from a much bigger and more beautiful one.

Pray today...

Father, I belong to You. Your house is my home. Help me to gain Your proper perspective on this time and place now while I move every day towards my true destination. Teach me to treat earthly things respectfully while understanding their true long-term value.

21

Smart Economics

> *Godliness with contentment is great gain, for we brought nothing into the world, and we cannot take anything out of the world.*
>
> 1 Timothy 6:6-7 (ESV)

Understanding the economics of Heaven will help you in many ways. Not only will it give you peace about your own finances, but it will give you a better perspective on what true wealth is.

For example: there are mobile phone games where players will spend hundreds and thousands of real dollars, even time and bodily health, to gain virtual assets within the game. A discontent of life can drive people to trade its wealth for temporary satisfaction in things that are less real. When the game is over, all that virtual gain is typically lost forever.

This same principle is true with spiritual wealth: godliness. The economy of Heaven shows that trading time and energy for satisfaction we cannot keep is as profitable as spending real money on virtual assets. But if you maintain contentment with what God has given you, if you cherish the fruit of the Spirit and understand that it is many dimensions higher than physical wealth, then you will be satisfied in life and receive great gain.

Pray today...

Heavenly Father, thank You for all your gifts and fruits. I understand that the wealth of the Kingdom is of a higher dimension and value than what the world thinks wealth is. Teach me godly contentment, to breathe deep and know what is truly worth my time and energy.

22

No Compromise

So whoever knows the right thing to do and fails to do it, for him it is sin.

James 4:17 (ESV)

There is a corollary we can extend from the above scripture: that whoever is tempted with the wrong thing to do and refrains from it, for him it is righteousness. Resist the Devil, and he will flee from you and your newfound authority.

One key to walking in peace and simplicity is to know the ground rules for what you do not compromise on. The world often tells us, "Don't compromise your personal convictions," but there are two problems with this: first, your principles can change from one day to the next; second, who is going to support you when your principles are purely your own?

Instead, we need a set of convictions that are unchanging, and owned by someone with the power and authority to help us in times of conflict when standing fast means also standing against. Knowing what contradicts God's Word and refraining from it is righteousness, but also it will provide peace because you can always be sure that your motives are pure, and God will help you, even if others do not understand.

Pray today...

LORD, I find my peace in being able to make decisions simply. Your commands and promises always come first and are the one thing I won't compromise on, with everything else coming second place. Please keep teaching me Your Word so that I can make godly decisions.

23

Let It Go!

> *"For if you forgive other people when they sin against you, your heavenly Father will also forgive you."*
>
> Matthew 6:14 (NIV)

Have you ever heard the phrase "You cannot outgive God"? It's often used with regards to financial generosity, but the principle is the same with all acts of giving. God will not – cannot – be outdone in acts of mercy and love.

All through the Gospels we are reminded by Jesus that the amount of grace we extend to others will be the baseline for the amount of grace we can expect to receive from God himself.

So if someone wrongs you, let it pass. If they fail you, don't keep bringing it up. Learn the times when hurt needs to be amicably addressed in order to mend relationships, versus the times when a simple act of forgiveness is enough for someone's mistake.

By living with arms open toward others, you set the baseline for God's own arms to be constantly open toward you. And who wouldn't want to live completely saturated in the generosity of God?

Pray today...

Father in Heaven, hallowed be Your name. May Your kingdom come, and Your will be done. Give me all that I need for today and forgive all my mistakes, just as I choose to forgive anyone's mistakes against me.

24

Refreshing Repentance

Blessed is the one whose transgressions are forgiven, whose sins are covered.

Psalm 32:1 (NIV)

Psalm 32 depicts David's journey from a place of heaviness and wasting away to one of blessing, which he ties to a progression in his own soul from silence to repentance. As he confesses his sins before the LORD, he receives forgiveness, and with it a sense of divine refreshment.

Confession is something we all need to practise more of, both to God and to each other. It is too easy to keep our faults and sins inside, hoping they will disappear by themselves, while all the time we feel God's heavy hand upon us.

Peter backs this up in Acts 3, exhorting the crowds to repent and let their sins be washed away "so that times of refreshing may come from the presence of the LORD". The Devil will try every fear and lie to keep you from being set free and refreshed, but the truth is that when you come before God and honestly confess your incapability, He will wash you clean once again and show you His full capability.

Pray today…

Father God, I am sorry for the sins I have been keeping from You and from others. As I become aware of them right now, I confess the areas where I have missed the mark, and ask for Your forgiveness. I receive Your forgiveness as You wash me clean, so that I may start afresh.

25

Faith Like Flowers

"I tell you the truth, unless a kernel of wheat is planted in the soil and dies, it remains alone. But its death will produce many new kernels—a plentiful harvest of new lives."

John 12:24 (NLT)

Have you ever considered that God created plants to naturally produce faith? A flower typically cannot sprout a new plant from itself, it must first let go of its seed and leave it in God's hands. That a seed must die in order to live is pure faith by nature on the part of the plant.

It might be strange to think that flowers have faith, because they clearly have no mind or spirit, by which to choose. But this simply demonstrates the kind of faith that the LORD wants us to learn: faith by nature.

Letting go of seeds does not mean to disregard them. There is a big difference between nonchalance and open-handedness. A plant grows first with its bud closed, and then opens up to allow the seeds to fall.

Whatever you have been nurturing, be ready and willing to allow it to be set free. This will almost always mean trusting God with your seed, even when it looks like death. Understanding the seasons of life means to be able to rest in letting go, knowing that it is a natural cycle of nurturing, falling and then new life with multiplication. Let your faith be like flowers.

Pray today...

Heavenly Father, I place my seeds and the fruit of my life in Your hands. Teach me to be diligent with what I have been entrusted with, but also open-handed and aware of the seasons of falling and of new life.

26

God is There in Your Darkest Place

Where can I go from your Spirit?
Where can I flee from your presence?
Psalm 139:7 (NIV)

Psalm 139 has often intrigued me. Such a beautiful, poetic song is seemingly spoiled toward the end by a sudden outburst of anger by the writer. Couldn't he have been more sensitive? What was the point?

All through the psalm, we are building up a case study of the presence of the Holy Spirit; where He dwells and what He knows. The psalmist presents dark places, secret places, faraway places, yet none of them too obscure or too far for God's presence to be found there.

Then, in a surprising burst of rage, he reveals the state of his heart: full of anger at the enemy and the unrighteous. And finally – having deduced that no place is too dark or too deep for God's presence – he invites the Spirit of God to enter his enraged heart and search its own depths.

Here is the encouragement: no matter how far you go, how dark the storm, how deep inside your heart you are carrying hurt, there is nowhere too far from the Holy Spirit. We might imagine God as the Prodigal Son's Father waiting for us to take a long journey back home, but actually as a carrier of the Holy Spirit, the home is right there within you.

Pray today...

Spirit of God, search me now and know me intimately. Thank You that we are never too far apart. My heart is Your home. See if there are any wicked tendencies in me and lead me in the way everlasting.

27

The Best-Laid Plans

*Commit to the LORD whatever you do,
and he will establish your plans.*

Proverbs 16:3 (NLT)

The famous novel *Of Mice and Men* quotes an old Robert Burns poem which teaches that "the best-laid plans of mice and men often go awry". There is truth there; if a man in his fallible nature tries to work out his own plans there is a good chance that things will turn out badly.

However, the Bible teaches us a better truth: that the best plans are actually committed to the LORD, and with Him guiding and laying our steps they do not go wrong.

The proverb does not mean that you simply tell God whatever you desire, and He helps you get it. Our job is not just to keep the LORD informed of our plans, but to commit them wholly to Him. That means that You are trusting God with full permission to redirect or improve your vision.

How does this connect with peace? When your heart's desire is that God directs your steps and is fully involved, then if any doors start closing or things don't go according to your original plan, you can have peace knowing that this is the LORD guiding you; if perseverance is needed or a fight is coming, you can be sure that He is going to direct you accordingly.

Pray today...

LORD, I commit to You all my plans for today and for the future. I have made my plans, but You will guide my steps, and I'm looking for full partnership with You to help establish our plans in the best way.

28

Friendships, Not Followers

> *One who has unreliable friends soon comes to ruin, but there is a friend who sticks closer than a brother.*
>
> Proverbs 18:24 (NIV)

Everyone knows how good it is to have friends, and God also wants you to be blessed with great friends. But if you really want to pursue a restful life, your friendships need to be rich in quality, not in quantity.

In this age of social media, the world teaches us that the goal for a successful life is to have as many followers as possible – often with a view to monetize them. We can too easily get into the dangerous game of living off likes and comments, momentary bursts of affirmation for our identity that wear off quickly and can even become an addiction.

Followers and likes may make you feel good for a moment, but Proverbs teaches that without true friends who are like family, without deep friendships built over purposeful quality time, you run the risk of either burning out or going down in flames.

Cultivation often starts just with being intentional. Consider one or two good people in your life that you can start meeting with regularly and simply share life's ups and downs. The results may refresh you.

Pray today...

Holy Spirit, You are the definition of fellowship, a perfect companion who sticks closer than a brother. I want to be more like You, so please help me develop the gift of fellowship. Teach me to value quality over quantity, and to search for the gold in godly friendships.

29

Let the Anointing Flow

Behold, how good and how pleasant it is for brethren to dwell together in unity! It is like the precious oil upon the head, running down on the beard, the beard of Aaron, running down on the edge of his garments.

Psalm 133:1-2 (NKJV)

The Bible stresses how important it is for us to pray for all leaders from the highest to the lowest point of office. Authority is a God-ordained concept, and as Paul writes in 1 Timothy 2:2, praying for our kings and rulers helps us to live peaceful and quiet lives of holiness.

Anointing oil is a symbol of governmental and spiritual authority. When kings and priests were appointed, oil would be poured on the top of their head, where it would then flow down over their clothes. Notice that anointing oil always flows down from the head, the highest place of office, to the rest of the body. As the head is anointed, so the body is.

Oil also represents goodness, peace and unity as we see in Psalm 133. So, if you desire to see more goodness and peace in your life, pray for your leaders. Whether it is a pastor, a boss, or a politician, recognise that all authority – no matter how well or badly it is wielded – is God's creation. Bless it, pray for those with it, and let the anointing flow down.

Pray today...

LORD, I recognise that You created authority; it is a godly thing. So I speak blessings over all my leaders; may they be filled with wisdom and godliness, to wield authority well and bless those they are anointed over.

30

Watch and Learn

The things which you learned and received and heard and saw in me, these do, and the God of peace will be with you.

Philippians 4:9 (NKJV)

Do you have a mentor? Is there someone you respect in the Faith that you can talk to, learn from, listen to, and grow under? Of course, we should all be disciples of Jesus first and foremost, but He also has given us apostles, prophets, evangelists, pastors and teachers, all purposed to build up His body.

If you want to receive more of the God of peace, one very good thing you can do is to find someone rich in wisdom and spirit and become intentional in watching and learning from them. If that begins with reading books and watching videos, it's a fine start, but do not discount the presence of real mentors in your life and in your home.

God created humanity with the incredible ability to be very adaptable. Whomever we spend time around watching and learning from, we start to become more like; it simply cannot be helped. So consider today who those people are in your life, and if there are others you would love to use as a template for your growth.

Pray today...

Holy Spirit, I recognise the importance of good teachers in my life. I know that You first always teach me of Jesus, but I also ask You to bring great mentors around me, and to increase the godliness I can receive from those already in my life. Help me to grow well, as I watch and learn.

31

Eat, Drink, Be Merry

> *"The Son of Man, on the other hand, feasts and drinks, and you say, 'He's a glutton and a drunkard, and a friend of tax collectors and other sinners!'"*
>
> Luke 7:34 (NLT)

Jesus drove the Pharisees mad; they couldn't understand how someone so full of power could have the sheer audacity to enjoy life so well. The temptations of this world had no grip on Jesus, because His heart was already filled with the Father's love, therefore He had all the freedom to sit at any table (that he wasn't flipping) and share good times.

People have different opinions on the consumption of alcohol, and perhaps the more important thing to note here is that Jesus clearly wasn't a closet drinker or an insatiable eater. His reputation of being a "glutton and drunkard" was linked to being a "friend of sinners". In other words, his enjoyment of food, drink and entertainment was directly connected to his enjoyment of being with and loving people.

Fun is not an evil force in itself, although it can become a desire of the flesh. God knows the best way for us to enjoy this life, and it is often more about the people we share the moments with than what the moments are. Set up regular times to get around a table with others and have fun!

Pray today...

Jesus, show me the keys to having a joyful life, full of enjoyment and fun, and sharing it with those around me just as You would. You're such fun, and were never compromised by the world – teach me to be just like You!

32

The Karma of Queuing

> *"But when you are invited, take the lowest place, so that when your host comes, he will say to you, 'Friend, move up to a better place.' Then you will be honored in the presence of all the other guests. For all those who exalt themselves will be humbled, and those who humble themselves will be exalted."*
>
> *Luke 14:10-11 (NIV)*

One of the British cultural idiosyncrasies that I have grown up with is that national pastime we call queuing. The Brits are excellent at knowing their place in a queue, owning it, maintaining it, and making sure everyone else knows their own. This is basically effective as it enforces sensitivity by ostracizing any attempt to try to jump the queue.

The problem with queuing is that it's a form of karma, as it teaches us that everything must be fair, and that fairness is a human right. And the problem then with fairness is that the moment the scales are imbalanced, and your place is lost, frustration and anger quickly rise up.

Jesus shows us the better way: relinquish fairness and allow others to be honoured before you. Then it is impossible to lose anything, and better yet, you will see the gift in times when grace is extended back towards you. Let others have your place; trade up queuing for grace.

Pray today...

Dear Jesus, forgive me for when I have sought after fairness, and tried to hold on to my position, instead of freely giving it to others. Just as You stepped down from Heaven to love others, teach me to do the same.

33

Living for Today

"Therefore do not worry about tomorrow, for tomorrow will worry about itself. Each day has enough trouble of its own."

Matthew 6:34 (NIV)

God is ageless and timeless; as the God who was, who is, and who will be, He is not bound to a single realm of time. As for us, God created a special time that we are allowed to inhabit and experience, which is today. We may wonder about the future, or remember the past, but neither are realms that we were designed to inhabit or worry over.

God has given you everything that you need, and made you a conqueror through Christ Jesus, but for the realm that you were created to govern. If you take ownership of this day, you can make use of all that God has given you until He makes your enemies a footstool. But if you try to take ownership of both the present's finitude and the future's infinitude, you will quickly wear yourself out.

God is infinite, so He is specialised in handling the infinite possibilities of tomorrow and the days that follow. Give Him any battles for tomorrow, until it becomes today, at which point you can trust Him to give you all that you need to conquer it.

Pray today...

LORD God, thank You for giving me everything that I need to tackle today's issues and be an overcomer in each moment. I choose not to lose sleep over things that are outside of my realm and I place them all in Your mighty hands.

34

Pay Off Your Procrastination

No discipline seems pleasant at the time, but painful. Later on, however, it produces a harvest of righteousness and peace for those who have been trained by it.

Hebrews 12:11 (NIV)

The previous topic was about not interfering with the problems of tomorrow. This is now the second half: that we discipline ourselves to face the problems of today instead of ejecting them into the future.

We have all experienced the problem of procrastination, whether it is putting off homework, housework, office work, anything! And we have all experienced the anxiety that quickly grows from seeing problems pile up and fearing the consequences. Today's work was made for today, and you will receive the most peace when you tackle it during its allotted time.

If you have a problem with self-discipline in this area, it cannot be stressed enough how important it is to strive for breakthrough. If work is like finance, then procrastination is debt, and self-discipline is like paying off all your loans and credit cards. Start with something small today. Choose one task that you have been avoiding and make a commitment to pay that off today. When you've broken free from one debt, you will gain confidence for the next, and soon will receive the harvest of peace and righteousness that God promises all those who are disciplined.

Pray today...

Holy Spirit, give me strength and discipline to tackle today's problems today, not putting them off. You have given me everything I need for this day, so that I can face the job at hand with confidence.

35

Your Angelic Entourage

Then Elisha prayed and said, "O LORD, please open his eyes that he may see." So the LORD opened the eyes of the young man, and he saw, and behold, the mountain was full of horses and chariots of fire all around Elisha.

2 Kings 6:17 (ESV)

In the film adaptation of *The Lion, The Witch and The Wardrobe*, King Peter's righthand remarks that "Numbers do not win a battle," to which Peter wistfully replies, "No, but I bet they help!" There is something very reassuring – even energising – about having a mighty army on our side.

Here is the good news: God is never outnumbered or outmatched. The Father has all of Heaven's angels ready to stand between His children and the Enemy. No matter what situation you may be facing, those who are with you are more than those against you. Even the great dragon Satan in Revelation 12 was only able to sweep one-third of the stars, leaving him outnumbered two-to-one!

Elisha was a prophet of the LORD and able to ask for his servant to get an accurate vision of the situation. As a kingly priest filled with the Holy Spirit, and as one who belongs to the Good Shepherd, you yourself can ask the LORD for this same perspective at any time, even right now.

Pray today...

Father, help me see the true perspective of who is standing with me, beside me, all around me. No matter what comes, I can rest safe in the knowledge that You are my bodyguard, my shield, my fortress.

36

Refresh Your Memory

Remember the Sabbath day, to keep it holy.
Exodus 20:8 (NKJV)

Remembrance is a powerful force. Take the body and blood of Jesus as an example: every time we eat the bread and drink the wine, we are bringing the once-for-all event of His body and blood on the cross here into the present and refreshing ourselves with it. But not only do we receive the healing and forgiveness that extends from the cross, we also proclaim our faith in the future resurrection and the marriage supper of the Lamb.

This same power of remembrance happens every time we take a regular rest, switching off from work and focusing on refreshment with family. We are bringing the once-for-all event of the Sabbath Day here into the present, and we also proclaim our faith in the future Sabbath with Christ. Both have the power of restoration, which is activated in remembrance.

I expect that you practise remembering the cross of Christ when you come together with other believers to eat the bread and drink the wine. Try doing the same when you come together with your family for a regular day off. Take a moment to thank God for giving you the Sabbath; remember that it really is a gift, and that there is a future eternal Sabbath waiting for you along with all His children.

Pray today...

Thank You, God, for giving us the Sabbath since the very beginning, and setting it apart from all other times. I freely receive this gift and choose to practise it regularly in gratitude of what it means for now and forever.

37

A Table Awaits

You prepare a table before me in the presence of my enemies;
You have anointed my head with oil;
My cup overflows.

Psalm 23:5 (NASB)

If you were to imagine sitting down to eat while surrounded by your worst enemies, it doesn't sound like the most restful scenario. Your pulse would likely be racing, your eyes constantly checking for sudden movements. But right in this setting the psalmist David is fully at peace, because Almighty God is officialising His seal of approval on David's authority as king, with all his enemies as witnesses.

Whenever God establishes a covenant with His people, there is always a meal involved. Sometimes it is in the presence of friends with bread and wine to seal your unity, other times it is in the presence of enemies with anointing oil to seal your authority. But as David notes in Psalm 23, it is always the LORD who invites us to the table, who breaks the bread, pours the wine and anoints us with oil.

So if situations arise where the Enemy tries to bring unrest into your life, take a moment to remember that God has a table and a covenant for you. When you enter your prayer room and take your place at the table, it is the Enemy who feels unrest as the LORD establishes and anoints you.

Pray today...

LORD, I know that Your table awaits me, and it gives me confidence in the presence of my enemies. I receive your bread, your wine, and your anointing oil. I am confident in who You say that I am anointed to be.

38

Climate Change

Wake up, lyre and harp!
I will wake the dawn with my song.
Psalm 108:2 (NLT)

At the time of writing, my wife and I are very happy to be living in Lisbon, in a flat with east-facing windows that give us a wonderful view of the sunrise each morning. On a clear day, depending on the time of year, we get to see the sun coming up over the horizon, and it often has a positive effect on our outlook.

But what if you don't have such a blessed view each morning, or if the weather is bad? What if you live in a place where the weather is always bad? We can't rely on the sun to make us happy each day.

This psalm shows us that the shoe is actually on the other foot. Every morning, you have the ability to awaken the day and to set its mood, not the other way around. Unlike the elements, you have the free will to create spiritual weather through praise, worship and thankfulness, and to let that be the real climate change for the day.

So whether it is taking a "harp" or "lyre" (read that as piano or guitar), praying a prayer of gratitude, or playing worship music on speakers, you can choose each morning what you want the weather to be.

Pray today...

Thank You for this day, God. It is a gift from You, and I will see Your goodness in it. Every day, God, I will choose how to awaken the dawn; I will sing Your praises and create the climate change the day needs.

39

Creation's Testimony

But now ask the beasts, and they will teach you;
And the birds of the air, and they will tell you;
Or speak to the earth, and it will teach you;
And the fish of the sea will explain to you.

Job 12:7-9 (NIV)

It is clear that remembering God's greatness, His promises, and knowing that He is with us, is a great key to living a life of peace and rest. However, often the problem is that we simply forget God's goodness as we get caught up in the humdrum of work and in life's little distractions.

Psalm 19 tells us that the "heavens declare the glory of God", and Job also tells us that the animals and birds and the earth all teach us about God. All of God's creation is a living testimony to His power and goodness. It's interesting that in busy cities the wild animals are expelled, nature is replaced with concrete, even the stars disappear from light pollution.

Therefore, if you want to grow in remembrance of God, become intentional in regularly surrounding yourself with whatever will teach and remind you of Him. Find times to marvel at creation, observe the skies, pause and reflect more. These are more than just peaceful elements; they are witnesses of God's glory and will help to cement your knowledge of Him for the times you need it most.

Pray today...

Holy Spirit, help me to spend more time around things – as well as people – that are always reminding me of Your glory and goodness. Let me choose to look for things in nature that testify of You.

40

Silence!

The LORD will fight for you, and you have only to be silent.

Exodus 14:14 (ESV)

The Bible has a lot to say about not saying a lot. In our haste and anxiety, we can spill out all of our concerns and raise our voices to Heaven as loud as can be, even calling it intercession, yet Proverbs 29:11 tells us that a "fool gives full vent to his spirit, but a wise man quietly holds it back".

I do agree that there are times to declare God's promises in a loud voice, but the truth is that we as God's people need to practise silence a lot more than we currently do. We need to remember that the LORD fights for us, and that He consumes enemies with fire and a sword from His mouth.

Being silent is hugely important because it allows us to observe God, and to listen to Him. You will get an increased revelation of God when you stop speaking and start meditating on His Word, listening to His voice. You will also start partaking in this beautiful, divine conversation: listening to Him, then waiting on His silence knowing that He is also the one observing and listening to you.

If you don't normally engage in this, then as a practical example, just take thirty minutes of complete intentional silence. Ask the Holy Spirit in your heart what he wants to say or show you. Stop, observe, listen.

Pray today...

Holy Spirit, I choose right now to just be silent and listen to You.

Similar Book from the Publisher

Selah
Linda Daruvala
ISBN: 978-1-78815-610-3

'Selah' is a Hebrew word that appears in many of the biblical psalms. It is an instruction to the listener to pause and reflect on what has just been sung.

This spiritually nourishing collection of poetry was written as Linda Daruvala paused and reflected at Christian retreats and in places of stillness. From poetic paintings of God's creation to a Psalm-like outpouring of her heart to God, Linda echoes the experiences and emotions that are common to many of us in our journey with the Lord.

Available from all good bookshops
and from the publisher:

www.onwardsandupwards.org/**selah**